# THE *SMART* GUIDE

# TO PUBLIC SPEAKING

Michelle J. Dyett-Welcome

Smart Publishing House
Far Rockaway, NY 11691
www.smartpublishinghouse.com

*Dwain G. Welcome, Editor*

© 2008 Michelle J. Dyett-Welcome. All rights reserved.

No Part of this book may be reproduced, stored in retrieval system, or transmitted by any means without the written permission of the author.

First Published by Smart House Publishing 9/1/2009

ISBN 10: 0-9825400-2-7
ISBN 13: 978-0-9825-4002-2

Library of Congress Control Number: 2009909473

Printed in the United States of America
Far Rockaway, New York

This book is printed on acid-free paper.

# Table of Contents

**Acknowledgements** ..................................................................................v

**Foreword** ..............................................................................................vi

**Introduction** ........................................................................................vii

**Public Speakers promise** ....................................................................viii

**Chapter 1**
    Overview of Public Speaking ..................................................................1

**Chapter 2**
    Overcoming the Fear Factor ..................................................................11

**Chapter 3**
    Speech Organization ............................................................................22

**Chapter 4**
    What's Your Point? ..............................................................................34

**Chapter 5**
    The Best Way to Say It ........................................................................42

**Chapter6**
    How to be Your Best Critic ....................................................................51

**Chapter 7**
    What's Your Body Saying? ....................................................................58

**Chapter 8**
    Do You Have Vocal Variety? ..................................................................67

**Chapter 9**
    Research ............................................................................................73

**Chapter 10**
    Are Visual Aids Necessary? ...................................................................80

**Chapter 11**
    Do You Have the Gift of Persuasion? ...............................................86

**Chapter 12**
    Can You Inspire Your Audience? .....................................................97

**Chapter 13**
    How Well Do You Listen? ............................................................102

**Conclusion** ................................................................................110

**Bonus Section** ............................................................................112
    **10 Public Speaking mistakes you want to avoid...at all costs...**
    **9 Keys for Success**
    **The SMART Ah/Um Record**
    **The SMART General Evaluator**
    **The SMART Self-Assessment Review**
    **The SMART Timer's Record**
    **The SMART (Informal) Speech Evaluation Form**
    **The SMART Evaluation Speaker Form**
    **The SMART Speaker's Final Project Evaluation Form**

## Acknowledgments

I would like to thank God for the opportunity to write this book and for his favor in order to get it published. I thank the Lord for my family who supported, helped to proofread and edit the manuscript. May the Lord bless you for your love and encouragement.

# Foreword

As a public speaker, I know how challenging it is to overcome one's fear of speaking before an audience. The fear of public speaking according to surveys ranks higher than death! Any adult that wants to become successful in business needs to master the skills of public speaking.

This is the reason why I encourage my Speakers Cruise Free student's to join a public speaking group—so that they can learn how to present with confidence.

Michelle J. Dyett-Welcome was one of my former students. When I coached her she was apprehensive about speaking, but she was determined to make her dreams come true. She set out to overcome her fears and launch her business. She succeeded in spades and now has herself become a master.

Michelle's new book, *The SMART Guide to Public Speaking* is powerful tool for teens and adults. It is designed to teach pubic speaking in a simple straightforward manner to help the reader confront and overcome the myriad obstacles to a captivating presentation; a presentation that the audience enjoys and remembers!

*The SMART Guide to Public Speaking* is unique in how it helps the reader triumph over fear. There are some very astute and effective strategies here. Do yourself a HUGE favor, use them! You WILL be more proficient in public speaking and set yourself on the path of true public speaking success.

*Daniel Hall*

*Creator, "Speak on Cruise Ships: 8 Easy Steps to a Lifetime of FREE Luxury Cruises"*

*http://www.speakerscruisefree.com/*

# Introduction

Greetings Future Public Speaker,

I'm glad you decided to take action to address to your fear of public speaking. Many people including me have had to conquer their fear of speaking before an audience. The good news for you is that it can be done.

I can't promise that you'll never again have butterflies, but I can assure you that you will no longer want to throw-up or run from the podium or hide behind the lectern. You will have confidence in your ability to speak before an audience.

Don't believe it?

I understand your skepticism and your doubt. But you can overcome your fear of public speaking...and you will... **if you decide that you want to.**

In this workbook, you'll discover helpful lessons and exercises that will empower you to master the art of speech preparation—from selecting a topic, deciding its tone, writing the speech, organizing it, and practicing it.

All I ask... is that you fully give yourself over to the process of learning the techniques outlined in this workbook then make them yours. The truth is that in order for you to succeed at public speaking you have to be YOU!

Don't try to be Bill Clinton, Barack Obama or any other fantastic public speaker. Be yourself... Once you feel comfortable, doing this you'll be on your way to public speaking success.

I have also included in this workbook **10 mistakes** you want to avoid. If you avoid them, you'll catapult yourself to the top of the class.

If you're interested in improving your public speaking skills this workbook will help you hone your skills as it challenges you to raise the bar.

Here's to your public speaking success!

# The Smart Public Speaker's Promise

As an aspiring public speaker...
I promise to:

- Attend each class

- Come to class prepared

- Complete all exercises and homework assignments

- Practice my speeches

- Participate in class discussions and activities

- Offer constructive, honest and truthful feedback to my classmates

- Be open to the learning process

- Treat my fellow classmates with respect and courtesy

- Confront fear head on

# Chapter 1

## Overview of Public Speaking

*A people which is able to say everything becomes able to do everything.*

—Napoleon Bonaparte

**What is public speaking?**

The American Heritage College Dictionary defines public speaking as the act, art, or process of making effective speeches before an audience.

The art of public speaking goes back as far as man has been able to talk. It's the ability to communicate with others in a way they can comprehend and remember. Public speaking transcends cultures, continents, and economic barriers. Most people have to speak publicly at some point in their lifetime.

Public speaking isn't always formal it can be (an often is) informal. Each time you speak to a group of your friends or relatives you are speaking publicly. Once people are listening to you...you are a **public speaker**.

**What is public speaking really all about?**
Public speaking is one way you can share information with others. But it is more than just sharing information or facts. In order to be an effective speaker you need to engage your audience. Your goal is to capture their attention and hold it until you have completed your speech.

And it's not impossible to do...

You just need to know what to do in order to make this happen.

**What do Master Public Speakers know that you don't?**

**How do they grab their audience's attention?**

Master Public Speakers know how to captivate their audience. They grab their audience's attention from their very first word. There are many ways in which to do this. The use of a story or a joke can engage an audience. A quote or a startling statistic can also grab an audience's attention.

Have you ever heard a speaker speak and time seemed to fly by? This is what happens when an audience's attention is captivated. And this is what you're going to be able to do.

Professional public speakers use various techniques to gain the audience's attention—the key is knowing which one to use and when. But it goes further than that...it requires knowing your own...

**Strengths and Weaknesses**
Are you able to deliver a joke with the right punch? Are you a natural at story telling? Is facts and figures your thing? Are you an avid reader so you know famous quotes?

Knowing your own strengths and weaknesses is key to discovering your presentation style. To be a great public speaker you need to feel comfortable with yourself and your style. But in order to do that you need to be honest with yourself and know yourself.

**Know what your speech needs**
To be a successful public speaker you must also be able to assess what your speech needs. What will make it more creditable, believable, and memorable? Whatever you need to convey to your audience, in the way you intend should be in your speech from when you draft it.

Will you use everything that you have in your speech? Probably not. But it is better to have the information and not use it then to need it and not have it.

**Don't take yourself too seriously**
Don't get me wrong, I'm not suggesting that you not be professional. I'm suggesting that if you make a mistake, forget a line, or lose your place as you're speaking that you don't crucify yourself. It has happened to every public speaker at least once. Some of us more than that!

Just like a pianist, you don't have to stop and announce it to your audience you keep going. But if you really can't turn it around in your favor, tell your audience, "I simply hate when that happens...I've lost my place, and I so wanted to impress you all."

Then laugh it off and find your place. A little sense of humor helps to put everyone at ease.

**Be Prepared**
Before you start to write your speeches ask yourself some questions and determine your speeches objective. Ask yourself the following:

- What is your presentation style? Interactive (group participation), question and
 answer or lecture.
- What's the tone of your presentation?
- What are your audience's emotional triggers, needs, wants or desires?
- Who is your audience? Are they preachers, lawyers, home-school moms, colleagues or friends...?
- What do they need from you? To be entertained or informed?
- What is it you want them to walk away with? Social consciousness? Morality? A new product that will make their lives better?
- What is the purpose of your speech? Is it to entertain, motivate, inspire or to inform?

This is not a conclusive list, but it will help you to start thinking about the purpose and the goals you would like to achieve with your speech. Once you have this information, you will start to get a picture of how best to approach your audience.

You see... each group has different triggers (emotional pulses) and as a speaker, you need to know this in advance so you can set their triggers off.

Why? Because if you can engage them on an emotional level they will pay attention. They will do or learn what it is you want them to. And that is the purpose of public speaking.

If you fail to engage your audience or to set off their triggers, it will make your job much harder if not impossible to accomplish.
If you can answer these questions concisely and completely you are well on your way to preparing a good speech.

**Be Observant**

An important aspect of public speaking is observation. Look and listen to what your audience is saying to you though their questions and though their body language. And if possible address what you are observing in your speech. You can simply ask "are there any questions?"

If you are unable to do this because of the type of speech or the presentation format. Let your audience know that if there are questions you will be available to answer them after your presentation.
The truth is even with all of this preparation you could still lose your audience…

Why?

If you don't listen to them when they are speaking to you.

Your presentation may be in the form of a lecture and your audience may ask questions by raising their hands or by the expressions on their faces. How you address this will determine whether you are effective or not.

Suppose your audience can't ask questions because of time constraints. Can they still talk to you?

Yes, through their body language. It is your job to read their body language. Are they alert, excited, yawning, or restless? Are they wearing puzzled looks on their faces?

Your objective is not to have your audience confused, frustrated or bored. You want your audience to understand you… to be enthused…to be alert.

What can you do if your audience is going to sleep or appear to be bored? This is a great time for humor. If the subject matter of your speech doesn't lend itself to humor you can acknowledge the fact that this is difficult material.

# Overview of Public Speaking

The truth is that you have to be creative in how you respond to what your audience is telling you.

## Be Clear
Above all else, you want to communicate your thoughts clearly and completely. Take the time to develop your thoughts. Be sure to take your audience through the points you're making, logically.

You don't want your audiences' reaction to be "huh."

You want them to say, "Yeah I follow that. I agree with that. Or that makes sense."

Within this process, you can utilize other tools in order to make what you're saying clearer.

## Other tools that you can use:
- Handouts
- Displays
- PowerPoint
- Sound effects
- Samples (things your audience can touch/smell)

In chapter 10, we will explore in detail why you should use these tools and how they can help you capture your audiences' attention.

## Summary
There are several components to being a good public speaker.

## Preparation (ask questions)
- Determine your objective
- What is your presentation style
- What's the tone of your presentation
- Who is your audience
- What are their emotional triggers, needs, wants or desires

## Be Clear
- Express complete thoughts

**What is your audience saying to you?**
- Body language
- Questions that they ask

# Chapter 1 Classroom Exercises

Since this is a course in public speaking you will have many opportunities to flex your public speaking muscle. Throughout the course you will be asked to give impromptu speeches. You will be given a topic of discussion and timed.

This is not intended to scare you but to build up your confidence. You will not be asked to tell us who was the first man on the moon or who first invented the light bulb. But you may be asked to tell us who you love most and why...in two minutes.

(Ideally we would like each student to be able to complete each assignment in front to their classmates. But this is dependent on time constraints and the number of attendees per session.)

**Assignment 1**
(Write your answers in the space provided)
In one to two minutes, tell the audience about yourself.




**Assignment 2**
(Write your answer in the space provided)
Tell your class what you have learned and what you think about your first class. You have a maximum of two minutes in which to do this.

**Assignment 3**
(Write your answer in the space provided)
What are your strengths and weaknesses? (List as many as you feel comfortable listing).

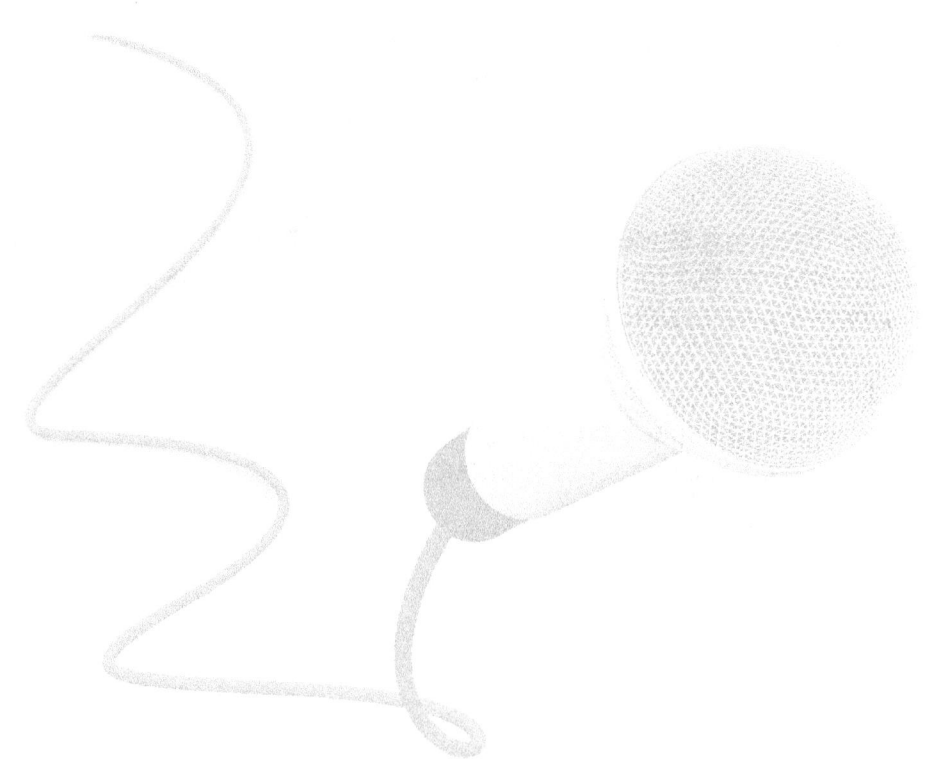

## Chapter 1 Review
Let's review what you've learned in this chapter so far.

**What are some of the things you should know if you want to become a Master Public Speaker?**

**What is the definition of public speaking?**

**What is public speaking really about?**

**What does public speaking mean to you?**

## Homework 1

I would like you to take a few minutes and think about what really makes you frightened when you think about public speaking. Make a list of the top five things. If you'd like you can list more.

If you are serious about overcoming your fear of public speaking or you want to use your nervous energy to your benefit then you should do each assignment. This workbook is designed help you learn through honest discovery.

### Preview

In chapter 2, you will discover how to overcome the fear factor and in chapter 3 you will learn about speech organization.

# Chapter 2

# Overcoming the Fear Factor

*Speech is always bolder than action.*

—Johann Fredrich Von Schiller

When you think of speaking before a group of people does your stomach feel sick? Does your mouth get dry? Does your mind go blank?

If any of these things happen to you, you are not alone. I also experienced some of these symptoms. That is one of the reasons I decided to work on my public speaking skills. I didn't like feeling scared.

And I will bet that is one reason you decided to take this course. You want to overcome the fear factor.

In this chapter, you will discover a few techniques that will help to reduce or control your fears.

**Know Thy Subject**
It is helpful to pick a topic or a subject that you know or that you are interested in. This will allow you to use a conversational tone or to be able to share your own story.

**The Art of Practice**
*Mirror Rehearsal*
Truthfully there is no better way to confront your fears then to practice. Familiarity with your subject matter and your speech will help you to feel comfortable and confident.

Practice your speech several times in front of a mirror. Observe your movements. Is your face relaxed? Are your hands flying out of control? Are you ringing your fingers? The object is to be comfortable as you recite your speech in front of your mirror.

Revise your speech if it is not sounding or flowing as you would like it to.

### *Family or Friend Rehearsal*
Once you feel comfortable with the subject matter and with giving the speech, it's time to go live. Practice your speech in front of your family or friends. If you can't handle presenting your speech in front of a large group yet, try it in front of one person. Then gradually increase the numbers.

Remember your family and friends are on your side and they want you to do your absolute best. Ask them to rate you and to give you feedback on how you can improve. Keep in mind that you can accept or reject their suggestions, but I would advise that you at least consider them.

Ask them questions. Did they enjoy the speech? Was it clear? Is there anything that you should leave out? Should you elaborate on anything? This will help you gauge the response of your prospective audience.

At this stage you should revise anything that causes confusion or is not clear to your audience.

### *Rehearse without Notes*
Once you have practiced in front of a group several times, try to give your speech without notes. Note if you remember the most important information from your speech. If you are able to do this then you may be ready to give your speech just using an outline.

If you can't remember your speech then you're not ready to give the speech without your notes and that's alright. It takes some people longer to feel comfortable giving up their notes, and I'm one of them. While my husband can give speeches straight from his head.

Keep in mind that you want to be yourself and you want to be comfortable. If you are not ready don't put pressure on yourself to present as you have seen others do it. If you have a deadline that is putting additional pressure on you...try to look at the presentation as a learning experience this will help to alleviate some of the pressure. It doesn't have to be perfect—you are just trying to learn.

Again as you practice your speech refine and revise it as necessary. There will come a point when you have done all you can do to your speech. When you know that you have reached that point...stop editing because you are in danger using the revisions as a way to procrastinate.

**Know your Audience**
We will discuss this in more detail in chapter 3, but for now note that it is important to know your audience. If possible go out and meet them. Visit the places they visit. Shake their hands. Study them (their interests, hobbies, problems) before you prepare your speech and definitely before you present your speech.

This will help you to feel more relaxed around them because they are no longer a group of strangers. You have gotten to know some of them by name and you have a face that goes with that name now. This may not be possible in every instance, but if you do proper research you can be confident that you know them for you will understand what they need most and you can address that in your speech.

**Try some Yoga**
Whether you are into yoga, breathing exercises or simple stretches use them to help you relax. Take a few minutes before you give your speech to release your tensions. Use your nervous energy to your advantage—transform it into enthusiasm.

**The Art of Visualization**
When you were young did you ever imagine you would be the President or a policeman? Didn't it seem real?

Well, why not imagine yourself giving your speech. See yourself delivering it with power, conviction and enthusiasm. Picture yourself beginning and closing your speech with a bang. Envision the positives. Envision what you will say or do if something goes wrong.

This will help you to be able to respond spontaneously and it will also help you to see that if something does go wrong you will still be alive. The truth is that visualization can help to boost your confidence. And if you have confidence it's hard to be consumed with fear.

### Arrive Early and Check the Place Out
Be an early bird. Get to the room early—check the equipment, the acoustics and your visual aids. This will allow you time to solve any problems that may arise.

### Your Audience is on Your Side
I know this is hard to believe, especially when you have hundreds of eyes staring at you. But nonetheless it is true. Your audience is on your side. They want to hear what you have to say. They want to learn from you, be motivated by you, be inspired through you or they want to be entertained by **YOU**.

So why wouldn't they be on your side? They came there to benefit from your speech. If you fail then they did not gain anything.

### Never Say "I'm Sorry..."
I know this is a hard one...but please refrain from saying, "I'm sorry, I'm just nervous." This is a big no, no.
Your audience probably will never know that you are nervous unless you say so. So why bring it to their attention? Why cause them to have to worry about you being able to get through your speech? Why make them responsible for your nervousness?

### Don't Upstage Your Speech
This may be hard to understand but the truth is you don't want to shift the focus from your speech to yourself because of your gestures or inappropriate attire. You want your audience to focus on the message. When you prepare your speech you should have a purpose and objectives you want to achieve—let that be the focus.

### Experience Teaches Wisdom
The more you speak the better you will become. You will learn what works and what doesn't. You will develop the skills to read your audience. You will learn how to use humor, when to use hand jesters, when to change your tone, when you should emphasize certain words or when to repeat a phrase for effect.

Experience builds confidence and it reduces fear.

## Face Your Demons

Everyone has internal demons that at some point in life they will need to face if they want to get free. It could be timidity, speaking anxieties, social encounters or confrontation issues...but whatever it is at some point you will need to face it if you're to break free from it.

And this is what you are going to do as you face your fears head on in this course. Fear can't win unless you decide to do nothing.

# Chapter 2 Classroom Exercises

### Assignment 1
(Write your answer in the space provided)
You a preparing a speech on health. How would you start your speech and grab your audience's attention?

### Assignment 2
(Write your answer in the space provided)
Tell your class what types of speeches you are interested in doing or the type of speeches you usually deliver? You will have one to two minutes in which to do this.

### Assignment 3
(Write your answer in the space provided)
Can you remember a time that you made a slip while you were speaking publicly? (If you haven't, have you thought about what that would be like?) Describe it. Tell what you did or what you will do.

## Assignment 4
List two things that you hope your classmates learned about you from your speeches.

## Assignment 5
List three things that you learned about your classmate from their speeches.

Are you wondering why we asked you to list what you learned from your classmate's speeches?

The reason is simple. Part of being an effective communicator is being able to listen. As well as knowing what it is that you want your audience to walk away with. We will discuss this in more detail in chapter 13.

## Chapter 2 Review

Let's take a few minutes to go over what you learned in chapter 2.

1. **What are some of the strategies you can use to help you overcome fear? (List as many as you can.)**

2. **What role does practice play in dealing with fear?**

3. **How can experience help you to overcome fear?**

4. **What are some things that you can do to help you relax before you give a speech?**

5. **Why should you arrive at the room early?**

# Homework 2

**Assignment 1**
Review the speeches that you wrote for your class assignments. Rewrite them the way you really wish you had written them in the first place. Keep in mind your objective and purpose of your speech. Think about who your audience is.

**Assignment 2**
Now I want you to list:

1. **What is your objective (s)?**


2. **What is the purpose of your speech (es)?**


3. **Who is your audience?**


4. **What do you want them to know or learn?**


**Assignment 3**
Write out what you would do if:

**A. The microphone goes dead.**


**B. There is feedback from the microphone.**

**C. The lights go out or flicker.**

**D. An alarm goes off.**

**E. People walk out while you are speaking.**

**F. Your visual aid falls down.**

G. **You trip.**

**H. A loud noise sounds.**

**I. Your PowerPoint presentation is upside down.**

## Self-Assessment Review 2

It's important to be able to assess your own presentations. You will not always get feedback from a relative, friend, classmate or an audience participant. You need to develop a habit of self-reflection and analysis. As a way of helping you develop this ability please answer the following questions.

1. **How would you rate your presentation on a scale of 1-10 (ten being exceptionally well)?**

2. **What are the mistakes you think you made?**

3. **What would you like to do better?**

4. **Did you communicate your point clearly to your audience?**

5. **Did your audience look engaged? Or confused?**

## Preview
In chapter 3, you will learn about speech organization.

# Chapter 3

# Speech Organization

*What this country needs is more free speech worth listening to.*

—Hansell B. Duckett

In this chapter, you will focus on speech organization. A good speech has a beginning, middle and an end. It should have a main message that you want your audience to take home.

In many respects it is like a story. It has a point to it. It doesn't really matter if it is a mystery, love story, fiction, true to life or a horror story. The point is that the story has a point.

In order for the writer to do this in the story he had to organize it and lay it out in a methodical way which would make sense—and engage the reader and to hold his attention to the end.

In essence this is what you will need to do as a speech writer. Yes, I did say speech writer. Because before you give a speech you should write it. And before you write it you should outline it.

What does this mean?

Let's look at developing a speech outline. In order to do this we will look at the questions you answered in chapter 2 homework assignment 2 and 3. Your target audience is home-schooling moms.

- **Who is your audience?**
- **What is/are your objective (s)?**
- **What is the purpose of your speech?**
- **What do you want them to know or learn?**
- **What emotional triggers do you want to press in your audience (if any)?**
- **What do they need?**

# Speech Organization

- **What should be the tone of your speech?**
- **What is your presentation format?**
- **Will you use humor? Or a story?**

In this chapter, you will explore each question and discover how answering them will help you to develop your outline and craft your speech.

## Who is your audience?
Your audience is home-schooling moms; therefore the information you will present to them would need to be of benefit or interest to home-schooling moms. What might be of interest to them?

You could give a speech on how to save money on school books? The best places to find bargains food? How to find a home-schooling support group in your area? How to be in compliance with state regulations as a home-schooling parent? How to get over the fear of teaching your child yourself? Or how about which home-schooling curriculum is the best for their child?

Once you know who your audience is then you can brainstorm or research what topics they would be interested in. Most groups have forums or discussion groups which you could join in order to see what their major pain, problem, question or interest is. And then you can set out to address it.

Again in order to address it you need to first define who your target audience is.

## What is/are your objective(s)?
Ask yourself what is it that you want to do. What is your objective? Do you want to inform? Entertain? Motivate? Teach?

Once you are clear on this you can then start gathering information or material that will help you accomplish your goals.

For this example let us assume you want to teach home-schooling moms how to deal with the fear of teaching their children. Let us say that most of them don't have a teaching degree or background...but they desire to home-school.

How would you encourage them? Allay their fears? How would you help them to develop confidence so that they can teach their child without fear or intimidation?

You can use a story or a testimonial of someone who has been through the same experience. Or you could share your own story provided you have had a similar experience. So you could use an example in your speech and have an inspirational and motivational component to it as well.

Once you are clear on your speech objective you can start to gather information that will help you to achieve your goal.

**What is the purpose of your speech?**
The purpose of your speech is similar to your objective. It really defines what you want your audience to go home with. If there is one key thing that you want them to walk away with… then this is what you would need to impress upon them.

And it could be a very simple point like "if I could home-school so can you." Or "everyone who first starts home-schooling has to overcome fear." Or "when you press pass fear you develop courage."

The point is that no matter what your take home point is it needs to be clear and memorable to your audience. So that if they don't remember the statistics, the jokes or the storyline they will remember the take home point.

**What do you want them to know or learn?**
As you explore what you want your audience to learn you would go back to your objective and the needs of your audience. This will help you to target the information you will provide for them. Does your audience need to know how many people per year try home-schooling? Do they need to know how many families dropout of home-schooling per year?

Do they need to know about support groups, frequently asked questions, obstacles that they may face, or challenges that they may encounter?

The way that you answer this question will determine what additional information or resources you will include in your speech. You may want to include support group resources and websites, will it be nationwide, international, or within the five boroughs and Long Island. Then you would do research to find this information.

## What emotional triggers do you want to press in your audience (if any)?

As you consider this question, you need to decide which emotions are at work in your audience. Earlier we stated that some of the moms may not have a degree in teaching so this may be a source of anxiety, fear or intimidation.

No!

You would want to give them courage and confidence. Again there are simple ways that you can do this. You can share with them the success rate of home-schooled students over students that attended public schools in the National Spelling Bee.

Or you can share a personal story or testimonial with your audiences in a way that helps them to picture themselves becoming successful at home-schooling.

### What do they need?
Earlier we touched on your need to discover what your home-schooling audience needs. Now you would need to define their needs in concrete terms. Do they need information? Do they need support? Do they need to be motivated? Do they need home-schooling skills? Do they need additional resources? Do they need an outlet to release their tensions and frustrations?

What do you think your audience needs the most? (You will have an opportunity to outline this later in your homework assignment.)

### What should be the tone of your speech?
The nature of your speech as well as your emotional involvement with the topic will affect the tone of your speech. If you are giving a presentation on an issue that you are passionate about like Evolution verse Creationism good tone would involve excitement, urgency and passion.

But if your topic is about how animals live in the wild your tone may be more contemplative, thoughtful, or reserved.

In chapter 8, we will look more closely at vocal variety in your speech, but for now it is important to note that your tone is influenced by how you feel about the topic as well as the topic itself. And this determines what your audience will hear when you present.

**What is your presentation format?**
What will your format be? In order to decide the format you should consider the following, who your audience is, who asked you to present and the amount of time you will have to give your presentation.

Would a lecture work best? A question and answer session? Or a group discussion? If the person who asked you to present has a definite presentation style in mind that will also help you make a decision.

Consider your time constraints. Will you have an hour or five minutes? The amount of time will influence the presentation style. For example a group discussion is more informal then a lecture as is a question and answer session. A lecture may not allow for lengthy group discussions. Neither a group discussion nor a question and answer session could be done properly in five minutes.

**Will you use humor? Or a story? Or something else?**
As you start to flesh out your speech you will decide whether story or humor will best illustrate the points you want to make. Your personality will also play a major role in what you choose to do as well as how you will do it. If you are not good at humor you would either avoid this style or you'd need to work on your timing.

If you're not a good story teller you would need to work on your story telling skills. It may be that your strengths lie in just sharing information with facts and figures, or using your personal experience as a way of connecting with your audience and that is okay.

No matter what you choose to do you want to be YOU. By being yourself you will be comfortable with the material you are presenting and that will come across to your audience.

# Speech Organization

**Beginning. Middle. End.**
Is your speech outlined with a beginning, middle and an end? Does it have a purpose, main ideas and points?
As you develop your speech it is easier to follow if you either follow the storyline approach...which includes a beginning, middle and end. Or if you use a logical approach where you have an overall purpose (objective), which is supported by ideas and illustrated with points (or examples).

By doing this you will be able to condense your speech and make it stronger without using unnecessary words and information. This will help your speech to be more effective.

# Chapter 3 Classroom Exercises

## Assignment 1
Take a few minutes to review the following questions:

**Who is your audience?**



**What is/are your objective (s)?**



**What is the purpose of your speech?**



**What do you want them to know or learn?**



**What emotional triggers do you want to press in your audience (if any)?**



**What do they need?**



**What should be the tone of your speech?**



**What is your presentation format?**



**Will you use humor? Or a story?**

# Speech Organization

Now you will have 2 minutes to develop a speech to target your home-schooling moms. You can focus on a need, problem or an area of interest you believe that they have. When the time is up then you will be asked to present your speech before the class.

**Assignment 2**
You are giving a speech to public speakers. What topic will you present to them? How would you organize the speech?

**What is your objective (s)?**



**What is the purpose of your speech?**



**Who is your audience?**



**What do you want them to know or learn?**



**Assignment 3**
**You plan to present a speech to the parents of your Sunday school class. What topic will you choose for your discussion? How would you organize your speech?**

**What are your objectives?**



**What is the purpose of your speech?**



**Who is your audience?**

**What do you want them to know or learn?**


**Assignment 4**
You are giving a motivational speech to salespersons. What topic will you choose to present? How would you organize the speech?




**What is your objective (s)?**



**What is the purpose of your speech?**



**Who is your audience?**



**What do you want them to know or learn?**

# Chapter 3 Review

**What information do you need to know or decide before you can properly draft an outline?**

1. What determines the tone of your speech?

2. What helps to determine your presentation style?

3. What are emotional triggers?

4. What are the different presentation styles that were discussed in this chapter?

# Homework 3

### Assignment 1
Go on the internet and Google home-schooling forums, articles or tips. Identify three problem areas that home-schooling parents face. (Save the site addresses.)

### Assignment 2
Go on the internet and research three areas that home-schooling parents are interested in. (Save the site addresses.)

### Assignment 3
Write a short speech that will educate, motivate or teach home-schooling parents in one of the areas you identified above. Please be sure to tell them where they can go to get additional information. If you quote from any author or site remember to give them credit in your speech.

## Self-Assessment Review 3

It is important to be able to assess your own presentations. You will not always get feedback from a relative, friend, classmate or an audience participant. You need to develop a habit of self-reflection and analysis. As a way of helping you develop this ability, please answer the following questions.

**How would you rate your presentation on a scale of 1-10 (ten being exceptionally well)?**

**What are the mistakes you think you made?**

**What would you like to do better?**

**Did you communicate your point clearly to your audience?**

**Did your audience look engaged? Or confused?**

## Preview

In chapter 4, you will learn about getting your point across to your audience.

# Chapter 4

## What's Your Point?

*Speeches that are measured by the hour will die with the hour.*

—*Thomas Jefferson*

In chapter 3, you learned about speech organization. Let us expand on this by analyzing how to make your point clear from the very start.

What is your point? Does it have a specific, well defined purpose? Let's examine this more closely. Once you have chosen your topic and have selected information you would like to include in your speech, then it is time to narrow it down.

For example, suppose your speech topic is about world history. This is a very broad subject area. Which century do you want to focus on? Want to focus on event—World World II or famous inventions? Which countries do you want to focus on, the United States and Japan? The United States and England?

Remember that you have a limited amount of time in which to give your speech. On average you will have 5-7 minutes (at most 30 minutes) unless you are in the teaching profession. Because of the limited time, you need to be as specific as possible. How can you do this?

First, define your general purpose. Do you want to inform, persuade, entertain or inspire with your speech? Next identify your specific purpose. This will help you to further narrow your topic. Be like a bird—though he sees many worms he only focuses on one to catch.

Let's look at a few examples on how to do this.

**Example 1**

**Topic:**               The West Indian Day Parade

**General Purpose:**     To inform

## What's Your point?

**Specific Purpose:** To inform my audience how the steel band prepares for the parade.

**Example 2**

**Topic:** How to Succeed at Home-schooling

**General Purpose:** Inspire/motivate

**Specific Purpose:** To inspire my audience so that they can overcome the obstacle of boredom in home-schooling.

Do you see how this works? Pick a general topic then you narrow it down to address one specific area. This will help you get to the point. And that is what you want to do.

Aside from being specific you want to be effective. Let us look at how we can make our purpose effective. Here are five tips to accomplish this.

### Tip 1
**Write a purpose statement as a full infinitive phrase (not a fragment)**
A fragment is an incomplete or isolated portion. To break or separate (something) into fragments.

While an infinitive is a verb form that functions as a substantive while retaining certain verbal characteristics and in English may be preceded by the word to.

What does this mean? As a non-English major I have the same question. It means to use the word to with a simple form of the verb with includes objects or modifiers. An infinitive phrase can function as a noun, adverb or adjective.

For example:
As a Noun: He helped *to write* the program.
As an Adjective: Lydia was looking for a way *to earn* money.
As an Adverb: He shouted *to get* our attention.

Infinitive phrases will increase the power of your speech.

### Tip 2
**Avoid Figurative language in your purpose statement**
This means you want to avoid flowery or colorful language. Or words like drag, bummer, messed up and the like. You want to keep the focus on what you want to accomplish and not on the words that describe your feeling about the issue.

### Tip 3
**Express your purpose as a statement not a question**
Questions make good headlines, or subject titles. But when you are developing your statement you want to flesh it out. State clearly what you intend to accomplish in the speech. This outlines where you want to go—and what you want your audience to know.

### Tip 4
**Limit your purpose statement to one distinct idea**
Have you ever heard a speech where the person was hopping from one idea to another? Did you get lost in the maze of ideas? Did you find it difficult to follow the speaker's trend of thought? Did you have a hard time understanding what his point was? If you have had this experience you understand why it is important to have one distinct idea.

### Tip 5
**Make sure your specific purpose is not too vague or general**
Again narrow your purpose down. Take out unnecessary words. Make it concise. If one word will do then use one word rather than two. If your topic is too broad then isolate one area of interest and focus on that.

Let's look at some examples.

**Example 1**

| | |
|---|---|
| **Ineffective** | To persuade my audience that registration procedures should be made easier and that credits for remedial courses should count towards graduation |
| **More Effective** | To persuade my audience that remedial courses should count toward graduation. |
| **More Effective** | To persuade my audience that the registration process should be simplified. |

## What's Your point?

**Example 2**
**Ineffective** — To persuade my audience that having to pay parking meters when you go to church is a real bummer.

**More Effective** — To persuade my audience to petition against the Mayor's plan that even on Sunday's meters have to be paid.

Are you getting the idea? The more specific you are the clearer your speech will be to your audience. There are a few questions that you should ask about your specific purpose.

Does my purpose meet my task? Can I accomplish my purpose in the time allotted? Is the purpose relevant to my audience? Is the purpose too trivial for my audience? Is the purpose too technical for my audience?

Why should you ask these questions? Simple, because you want your audience to benefit from your speech. If the speech is too technical and your audience lack the technical knowledge to follow your presentation—you will lose them.

If you talk down to your audience (trivial subject matter) they may feel insulted. If your subject matter is not of interest to your audience why would they pay attention?

As you develop your purpose both general and specific—consider your audience. What do they need? What information will be of benefit to them? How can you make it interesting to them? How can it be applied to their lives or situation?

Once you take the time to do this during the planning stage you are almost guaranteed that your speech will appeal to your audience.

# Chapter 4 Classroom Exercises

## Assignment 1
Review the topic below and write out your general statement and your specific statement.

**Topic:**  Weather Changes

## Assignment 2
Review the topic below and write out your general statement and your specific statement.

**Topic:**  Having a Pet is Good for People

## Assignment 3
Review the topic below and write out your general statement and your specific statement.

**Topic:**  Marriage in the United States

# Chapter 4 Review

1. Why is determining a specific purpose an important early step?

2. List the five tips for formulating your specific purpose.

3. Tell the difference between a specific purpose and a general purpose.

4. What are the five questions you should ask about your specific speech?

# Homework 4

## Assignment 1

Review the topic below and write out your general statement and your specific statement.

**Topic:** Cell Phones and Health

## Assignment 2

Review the topic below and write out your general statement and your specific statement.

**Topic:** Buying Your First Home

## Assignment 3

Review the topic below and write out your general statement and your specific statement.

**Topic:** Starting a Business

## Self-Assessment Review 4

It's important to be able to assess your own presentations. You will not always get feedback from a relative, friend, classmate or an audience participant. You need to develop a habit of self-reflection and analysis. As a way of helping you develop this ability please answer the following questions.

**How would you rate your presentation on a scale of 1-10 (ten being exceptionally well)?**

**What are the mistakes you think you made?**

**What would you like to do better?**

**Did you communicate your point clearly to your audience?**

**Did your audience look engaged? Or confused?**

## Preview

In chapter 5, you will learn the best way to say it.

# Chapter 5

## The Best Way to Say It

*Never try to impress people with the profundity of your thought by the obscurity of your language. Whatever has been thoroughly thought through can be stated simply.*

—Source Unknown

This is what it is all about for a speaker—using words accurately and correctly. You want to be clear, concise, accurate and correct. Be accurate in your pronunciation, correct in your articulation, and clear with your enunciation.

*Good speakers use words accurately and correctly (*Ellis Herwig/Stock, Boston).

**How to Use Language Clearly?**
A man has fallen overboard. What is the clearest way to say that? Is it not "man overboard?"

But you may find some who may prefer to say it in a lengthier manner, like "It seems apparent from the empirical evidence that a person has been thrust over the edge of the boat inadvertently, and has landed in the vast blue liquid environment in which sea creatures abide."

Which statement is clearer? The first one is. In your speech you want to use language clearly. Say what you want to say in the easiest and clearest way possible.

**Concrete Words**
In order to accomplish this you should use concrete words. Concrete words are specific. They are not general—they refer to people, places and things.

## Eliminate Clutter

Furthermore, you want to eliminate clutter. Take out any unnecessary filler words. Use strong verbs eliminate adverbs and adjectives that are redundant or don't breathe life into your speech. Think as you would if you were writing a term paper. You would state the facts; give examples of support, then your conclusion. That is what you need to do in your speech.

The last thing you want is for your audience to be archeologist—forced to unearth what you mean. If there is no way to say what you want to say clearly then utilize imagery if your speech lends itself to it.

Paint a picture with your words. Bring what you are saying to life. Be a novelist—create word pictures. That will allow your audience to understand what you are saying.

## Rhythm

Rhythm is not only used in music or poetry it can be used in speechwriting. The way that you put your words together can create a natural rhythm.—which you can exploit in order to touch an emotional cord in your audience. The ability to do this can enhance the impact of your words.

Martin Luther King Jr. and Winston Churchill were masters at this. If you have time take a look at their speeches. And if possible listen to them. It will give you an idea of how you can do the same.

I'm not suggesting that you deliver a speech like them but rather you learn from them. How they were able to engage their audience with the use of rhythm. You can even read the words from one of your favorite artists. How did they use the natural rhythm of their word to get you to pay attention?

## The Five Spices

As you develop your speech add some spice.

### Spice 1

Use quotes, stories, and anecdotes in your speech.

**Spice 2**
Use language that helps you to connect with your audience and establish a bond of solidarity.

**Spice 3**
Use vivid words this will help the listener to visualize what you are saying. It will paint a picture.

**Spice 4**
Use action verbs—to convey power.

**Spice 5**
Use positive words to encourage action.

Now that we have covered how to use language clearly and the five spices...let us look at delivery. Delivery has been defined as the ability to appear natural and poised when giving a presentation. But delivery is more than appearing collected. It is more than speaking with fluency; it encompasses the use of vocal cues (rate of speech, pitch, and volume quality), body language (such as hand gestures or distracting mannerisms), general physical appearance, and posture.

Speaking in a very low volume (whisper), very high volume (shouting), no use of hands (in the pockets), over-dramatization with the hands, very slow pace, very fast pace, don't look at anyone, look only at one person, these are all part of delivery.

We will go into more detail about proper body language and how to use vocal variety in chapters 7 and 8, but for now I would like you to be aware that each of these components has a direct effect on your ability to deliver an effective speech.

## Types of Speeches
There are many ways to deliver a speech. You can read from a manuscript, recite from memory, speak impromptu, or speak extemporaneously. The method you choose depends on you and your comfort level. As I shared with you before I use my notes—and on occasion I will speak impromptu, while my husband can speak from memory, impromptu and extemporaneously.

## Reading from a Manuscript
While it is true that certain speeches need to be delivered word for word it may not be true in your case. If you are the Pope, President, or giving a report at a professional meeting it would be essential that you are accurate and that you deliver your speech word for word. Especially if your words will be analyzed or if it could cause an international incident.

## Reciting from Memory
The ability to memorize a long speech and present it to the audience in a communicative manner is indeed a great achievement. If you can do this then by all means please do. But if you will have to stare at the ceiling or at the floor to remember where you were and what you wanted to say—you may want to stick with your notes or a simple outline. Trying to recall your message or to find your place will cause you to disconnect with your audience and them with you.

## Speaking Impromptu
Speaking impromptu is to speak without any immediate preparation whatsoever. Most speeches we have in our daily lives are impromptu. Do you rehearse before you talk to your family? A close friend? A teacher? No. Usually we just speak.

The problem comes when we have to speak impromptu before someone we don't know. Or in front of a boss or a group of people who may judge us. But as a Master Speaker you know that you should take time before you respond. Think about the question.

Then you can state the question that you're answering (you can paraphrase it). State the point you want to make—clearly. Support your position with the appropriate evidence—if you have evidence. Then summarize and restate your point.

## Speaking Extemporaneously
Speaking extemporaneously is when you prepare and practice your speech in advance yet when you give your speech you only use a bulleted outline (to jog your memory) or speak without notes. The exact words you use in your speech are chosen at the moment you deliver your speech.

## Pronunciation

Proper pronunciation is an asset in public speaking. For example many people mispronounce the following words:

| Word | Common Error | Correct Pronunciation |
|---|---|---|
| genuine | gen-u-wine | gen-u-win |
| err | air | ur |

If you were a teacher how important would it be for you to teach your student how to pronounce words correctly? If you were a politician how important would it be for you to say words correctly. It's understandable that sometimes people make mistakes because of nervousness. While others because they have simply learned the word wrong.

If you are unsure how to pronounce a word, just look it up in the dictionary. I have to use mine quite often!

## Articulation

Poor articulation is the failure to form particular words crisply and distinctly. Let's look at a few examples:

| Word | Misarticulation |
|---|---|
| ought to | otta |
| didn't | dint |
| want to | wanna |
| will you | wilya |

Does this convey competence? Does it make you sound credible? Will this tell your audience that you are knowledgeable?

You have to decide what you want to convey to your audience and then be deliberate about it.

As we discussed in chapter 4 you need to have a message. You need to know what your point is. Once you have determined what your point is then you can enhance your presentation with clear language, proper pronunciation, articulation and proper delivery.

# Chapter 5 Classroom Exercises

**Assignment 1**
Your boss whom you dislike is getting ready to retire and the person who was to present him a card and gift is out sick. You have been asked ten minutes before the speech is to be given to do it on the behalf of all the staff. What would you do? Write a sample speech for your boss.

**Assignment 2**
You are attending your friend's funeral. Everyone is giving speeches about how wonderful he was. One person comes up and reveals a well hidden secret about your friend. You are the next person scheduled to speak. Still reeling from the shock of the disclosure. What would you do? Write a speech that you would deliver.

**Assignment 3**
Create a list of words which you have difficulty pronouncing or articulating properly. Write a short poem or paragraph using these words in a rhythmic manner.

## Chapter 5 Review

1. **How can you use language clearly in your speeches?**

2. **What are the different ways you can deliver a speech?**

3. **Why is articulation and pronunciation important in giving a speech?**

4. **How does clutter affect a speech?**

# Homework 5

## Assignment 1
Write a short speech on any subject. Practice your delivery.

## Assignment 2
Think of a different topic. Give the speech impromptu in front of a friend or relative. If not possible record yourself doing it. How did you do? Evaluate yourself and ask your family member or friend to do the same.

## Assignment 3
Take the speech you developed in assignment 1. Memorize it. Now deliver it before your family or friend. If not possible record yourself giving your speech. Did it sound natural? Evaluate your performance and/or ask your family member or friend to evaluate you.

## Self-Assessment Review 5

It's important to be able to assess your own presentations. You will not always get feedback from a relative, friend, classmate or an audience participant. You need to develop a habit of self-reflection and analysis. As a way of helping you develop this ability please answer the following questions.

**1. How would you rate your presentation on a scale of 1-10 (ten being exceptionally well)?**

**2. What are the mistakes you think you made?**

**3. What would you like to do better?**

**4. Did you communicate your point clearly to your audience?**

**5. Did your audience look engaged? Or confused?**

## Preview
In chapter 6, you will learn about how to be your best critic.

# Chapter 6

# How to be Your Best Critic

*Man does not speak because he thinks; he thinks because he speaks. Or rather, speaking is no different than thinking: to speak is to think.*

—Octavio Paz

So far you have learned how to get to your point, the best way to say what you want to say. Now you will discover how to be your best critic. In the previous chapters, you were asked to do a self-Assessment review. Now we will expand on this concept.

What should you review about your speech? What should you pay attention to? Each word? Each gesture? Your breathing? Let's narrow down the scope of your focus.

In a nut shell you should focus on your non-verbal communications, delivery, preparation and your closing. In chapter 7, we will go into more detail on what is your body saying. But for now we will lightly touch on some key points.

In order to be an effective speaker you have to communicate with your audience through three major areas—nonverbal communications, your preparedness and your delivery. If you take the time to evaluate your speech before hand you will be well on your way to becoming a Master Public Speaker.

Let's look at nonverbal communication.

## Nonverbal communication
What are you saying before you start to talk?

**Dress for success.** Dress in a manner that will communicate to your audience that you are credible and that you are trustworthy. If you are giving a business speech then wear business attire. If you are doing a humorous speech and you need to dress a particular part then do that.

For example, one of my fellow public speakers was giving a humorous speech about exercising. She came dressed in exercise clothes for greater effect.

**Eye Contact.** Look at your audience. Let them know that you are confident.

**Smile.** Connect with your audience.
**Body Language and Posture.** Don't waste one opportunity to communicate with your audience. Use your body to show that you are confident and knowledgeable about your subject matter.

## Preparation
Preparation is being ready before hand. This is how are you'd demonstrating that you are credible, knowledgeable and an expert on you subject matter—by doing research, knowing your subject and outlining the objective of your speech.

**Organization.** Did you spend the proper time organizing your speech? Does your speech include strong evidence to support your position?

**Sound Reasoning.** Does your argument or position make sense? Does it follow logical reasoning?

**Define New Terms.** Did you include new or unfamiliar terms? Did you define, explain them and include examples?

**Empathize Key Points.** Does you speech empathize key points? Do you repeat them so that your audience will remember them?

**Clear Opening.** Is your opening clear, strong and gripping?

## Delivery
How well do you present your speech and yourself to the audience?

**Speed.** Are you rushing to get through your speech? Are you breathing normally? Are you taking time to pause?

**Enunciation.** Are your words clear? Or are they one long run on?

**Modulation.** Did you vary your pitch? Or are you speaking in a monotone voice?

**Emotion.** Does your speech incorporate emotion? Can you identify it?

**Generate Emotion.** Will it generate emotion in your audience? Is the emotional trigger strong?

**Strong and memorable close.** Will your audience remember your final words? Is it gripping?

Let's look at a simple evaluation form that you can use to critique your own speech before you go before your audience. The great thing about this evaluation form is that you can use it again after you speak. Plus you can have others use it to evaluate your presentation.

You may think that all the categories on the form won't help you if you are evaluating yourself. But you would be wrong. Each category can help you plan. What impression do you want to make on your audience? How can you best achieve it? How should you dress? Carry yourself?

As you review the evaluation form you will be forced to think about and answer these questions in advance. Remember the ability to deliver a great speech starts with great planning.

I recommend that you evaluate yourself at least two more times. Tape yourself and then listen to how you sound objectively. Videotape yourself and observe how your posture, eye contact, diction, and speed. Then have others evaluate you too.

Be open to learn. Be willing to make adjustments and to take suggestions. Once you are willing to learn you will.

Periodically reflect back on your speech…not to beat up yourself with "should haves" and "could haves", but to see what areas you can strengthen for maximum impact.

## Chapter 6 Classroom Exercises

**Assignment 1**
Is there any area on the evaluation form that you believe will give you difficulty? How will you address it?

**Assignment 2**
Write a two minute speech on any topic of interest. Present it to the class. Afterwards evaluate your performance.

**Assignment 3**
Observe one of your classmate's speeches. Evaluate his/her speech. Offer suggestions.

# Homework 6

**Assignment 1**
Make a video recording of yourself delivering your speech (if possible). Evaluate your presentation.

**Assignment 2**
Make a tape recording of one of your speeches. Evaluate your presentation using the informal evaluation form.

**Assignment 3**
Ask a friend or family member to evaluate you using the informal evaluation form.

## Chapter 6 Review

1. Why is it helpful to be your own critic?

2. How many times should you evaluate yourself?

3. List 3 ways in which you communicate with your audience nonverbally?

4. What are the three ways in which you let your audience know that you are an effective speaker?

## Self-Assessment Review 6

It's important to be able to assess your own presentations. You will not always get feedback from a relative, friend, classmate or an audience participant. You need to develop a habit of self-reflection and analysis. As a way of helping you develop this ability please answer the following questions.

1. **How would you rate your presentation on a scale of 1-10 (ten being exceptionally well)?**

2. **What are the mistakes you think you made?**

3. **What would you like to do better?**

4. **Did you communicate your point clearly to your audience?**

5. **Did your audience look engaged? Or confused?**

## Preview

In chapter 7, you will learn how you communicate with others though your body language.

# Chapter 7

# What is Your Body Saying?

*"Get in touch with the way the other person feels.
Feelings are 55% body language, 38% tone and 7% words."*

*—Author Unknown*

Now that we have explored how to be your own best critic. Let us take a deeper look at body language.

As you saw earlier, body language communicates with your audience nonverbally—through your posture, gestures, eyes, and facial expressions—and they all affect the way your listeners will respond to you.

Your nonverbal talk communicates more than what you verbally say. How many times have you noticed that what someone is saying is not what you are understanding from their body language?

The same is true when you are giving a speech. Your audience reads your body language.

**Personal Appearance**
The first thing that you will notice about a speaker is their appearance. How would you react if you were a member of Congress and the President came in to give a speech in his golf shorts? Or if you were an investor in the real estate market and your broker came in with ripped up jeans hanging down on his hips with no belt?

Would you want to hear what they had to say? Would you have confidence in them? I wouldn't. Every speaker is expected by their audience to exhibit a personal appearance in keeping with the occasion of their speech. They should be dressed appropriately.

# What's Your Body Saying?

In Stephen E. Lucas's book *The Art Of Public Speaking* he points out that "...personal appearance plays an important role in speechmaking." He also cites that "In a survey of top business executives, 84 percent revealed that their companies simply do not hire people who appear at a job interview improperly attired." The bottom line is...personal appearance matters.

## Gestures

Many speakers are concerned about their gestures. What should I do with my hands being the number one concern?

As a new public speaker you have so many other things to be concerned about like your topic, research, nervousness, overcoming fear, and engaging your audience. You should not spend too much time worrying about your hands. Here's a tip—whatever gestures you make shouldn't draw attention away from your speech or your message. Any gestures that you make should appear natural and fluid. Do not let your hands upstage your ideas.

Try to avoid ringing your fingers, turning your rings, fiddling with your necklace or buttons on your shirt. Don't crack your knuckles, or constantly comb your fingers through your hair. These actions are distracting and they will convey a message to your audience that you do not intend.

## Eye Contact

You should try to make eye contact with the entire room. Or at least appear to by scanning the room. Let your eyes convey confidence, sincerity and conviction. Let your audience know that you believe what you are saying and so should they.

Don't stare at your audience—this will convey hostility. Do not get frozen in one section of the room like a deer caught in a cars headlight—this will alienate parts of your audience and they will feel ignored. Don't stare at your shoes—this will signal tentativeness and that you are ill-at-ease. Or at worse that you are insincere or dishonest.

## Bodily Action

What should you do once you are in front of your audience? What should you do with your feet? How should your body look?

All speakers face these questions in the beginning. Nervousness can cause you to fidget with your papers, constantly shift your body weight from one foot to the other, to blink throughout your speech, to bob your shoulders up and down or to move back and forth on the stage like a perpetual-motion machine.

When you reach the lectern do not lean on it. Take your time to set your notes up and to relax. Take a deep breath or two. Give yourself time to set up the way that you want it. Stand. That's right stand still and quietly for a few seconds. Make eye contact with your audience. Smile—and release pent up tension. Make sure that your audience is paying attention. Then—and only then—should you begin to speak.

If you do this you will capture your audience by letting them know what you are about to say is important—that you are willing to wait until you get their full attention. Plus you have used the delay time to get your nerves under control. Not to mention the fact that you have established that you are confident in who you are and what you intend to say.

This will take you but so far. As you learned in chapter 5, you have to follow it up with a powerful opening and a meaningful speech. In chapter 11, you will learn how to persuade your audience using reasoning, evidence and emotion. But for now remember that you want to say the right thing but you also want to convey the right message through your body language.

## Chapter 7 Classroom Exercises

### Assignment 1
George is ready to give his first speech. He walks to the podium as if he is a man condemned to die by the guillotine. Throughout his speech he is fiddling with the buttons on his shirt. What is his body language communicating?

### Assignment 2
Sarah is giving her third speech. She is constantly staring at the left wall. What is her body language communicating?

### Assignment 3
George came into his staff meeting in a Hawaiian shirt and shorts. He is to give a talk on the merger plan. Which message will the audience hear louder and why? What impressions will he make on his audience? What would you do if you were in the audience? How would you react if you were his boss?

## Chapter 7 Review

1. **What are the ways in which you can nonverbally communicate with your audience?**

2. **What should you do when you first approach the lectern?**

3. **What does your audience expect from you—the speaker?**

4. **What role does personal appearance play in speechmaking? In getting a job?**

5. **What is the role of eye contact in a speech? What do you communicate to your audience when you fail to make eye contact with them?**

# Homework 7

**Assignment 1**
Watch a 10 minute segment of a news program with the volume off. Note what the anchors say with their dress, gestures, facial expressions, and the like. Write down what you observed.

**Assignment 2**
Watch a 10 minute segment of a drama program with the volume off. Note what the anchors say with their dress, gestures, facial expressions, and the like. Write down what you observed.

**Assignment 3**
Watch a 10 minute segment of a comedy show with the volume off. Note what the anchors say with their dress, gestures, facial expressions, and the like. Write down what you observed.

## Assignment 4
Compare your three observations from the above assignments. How do the nonverbal messages differ? Be prepared to discuss this in class.

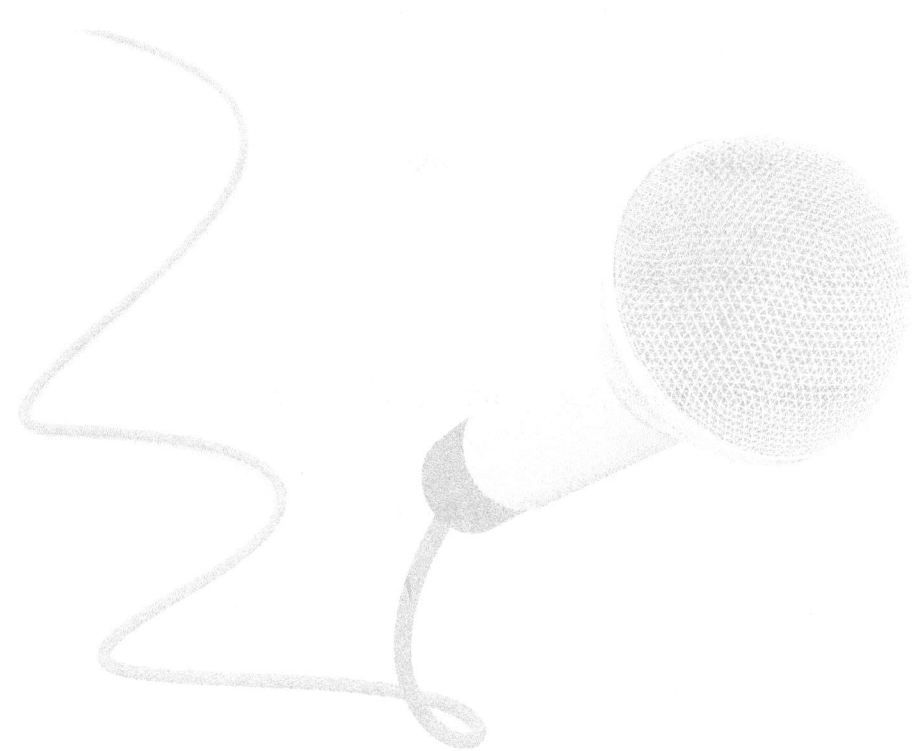

## Self-Assessment Review 7

It's important to be able to assess your own presentations. You will not always get feedback from a relative, friend, classmate or an audience participant. You need to develop a habit of self-reflection and analysis. As a way of helping you develop this ability please answer the following questions.

1. **How would you rate your presentation on a scale of 1-10 (ten being exceptionally well)?**

2. **What are the mistakes you think you made?**

3. **What would you like to do better?**

4. **Did you communicate your point clearly to your audience?**

5. **Did your audience look engaged? Or confused?**

## Preview

In chapter 8, you will learn about vocal variety.

# Chapter 8

# Do You Have Vocal Variety?

*Speech is the gift of all, but the thought of few.*

—Cato The Elder

Now that we have explored the various ways of delivery and what your body is saying, let's look at the power of your voice.

### The Power of your Voice
There are people who have a gifted voice. The tone and sound of their voice is soothing, powerful and lovely to hear. These individuals no doubt could have a career in voiceovers. I am not one of them. Or at least I don't think I am.

### Voice Type
What is your voice type? Is your voice deep and powerful like James Earl Jones or is it a high pitched and soft like Pee Wee Herman's? Whatever your voice type is, know that it is unique.

### Volume
Have you ever gone to a concert and the singer sounds like they are screaming at you? Or been in a church where the minister is yelling at you? I have. Sometimes I have had to plug my ears with tissue. Why does this happen? Often it is because the performer or speaker has not taken the time to adjust their pitch to match the acoustics of the room, the size of the audience, or to test the equipment in advance.

As a speaker you don't want to cause your audience to tune you out because the acoustics are echoing or amplifying what you are saying.

### Pitch
Pitch is the highness or lowness of your voice.

### Rate
Rate is the pace of your speech (the words that you speak per minute). Americans usually talk at a rate of 120 to 150 words per minute.

**Pauses**
Pauses are the brief breaks you take in between your words, sentences or statements. They can be very useful in a speech. They can signal the end of a statement, thought or they can be added for dramatic impact.

**Vocal Variety**
Vocal variety adds life and expression to your voice. You don't want to put people to sleep or bore them to death. Using vocal variety can ensure that you don't do either.

## Chapter 8 Classroom Exercises

**Assignment 1**
Take time to diagnose your speaking voice. Which aspects do you think need to be improved?

**Assignment 2**
Ask one of your classmates to diagnose your voice and you do the same for them. How does their assessment match with yours?

## Chapter 8 Review

1. What is pitch?

2. Why are pauses useful?

3. At what rate do most Americans speak at?

4. How can volume impact your speech?

5. Why is every person's voice unique?

# Homework 8

**Assignment 1**

Write a short speech on any subject. Focus on your vocal variety. Test two different ways of delivering your speech. Once with a monotone voice and the other with pitch and inflections. Remember to record yourself.

**Assignment 2**

Think of a different speech topic. Give the speech impromptu in front of a friend or relative. If it's not possible record yourself doing it. Test both of your chosen vocal variety methods. How did you do? Evaluate yourself and ask your family member or friend to do the same. Which one sounded better?

## Self-Assessment Review 8

It's important to be able to assess your own presentations. You will not always get feedback from a relative, friend, classmate or an audience participant. You need to develop a habit of self-reflection and analysis. As a way of helping you develop this ability please answer the following questions.

1. **How would you rate your presentation on a scale of 1-10 (ten being exceptionally well)?**

2. **What are the mistakes you think you made?**

3. **What would you like to do better?**

4. **Did you communicate your point clearly to your audience?**

5. **Did your audience look engaged? Or confused?**

## Preview

In chapter 9, you will learn the value of research.

# Chapter 9

# Research

*"Research is the backbone for an effective speech without it the speech is limp!"*

— *Michelle J. Dyett-Welcome*

In order to enhance your speech you will need to do some research on your subject. The best way to start is by compiling a list of what you already know on your topic. Then decide what information is missing. Research is the challenging part of speech preparation.

Keep in mind that as you do your research you want to gather information that will strengthen your speech—-like statistics, facts, examples. And you want to use stories, anecdotes, testimonies and visual aids that will help your audience picture what you are saying. (In chapter 10 we will go into more detail about visual aid use.)

The big question is how do you begin to do research? As I mentioned earlier you want to compile a list of the information that you already have. You want to organize this information so you can detect any gaps that may exist. The goal of your research is to plug in the gaps that may exist.

Where can you find information? The first place that you can check is your local library. But you can also check bookstores, college libraries or the internet. If you are searching the internet check more than one search engine. And try to narrow down your topic. If you have tried to do research on the internet you know that you can get hundreds to thousands of hits. You want to narrow it down so that the information found is more closely matched to your objective.

**Keys to Good Research**

**Start Early:** don't wait until the night before your speech to do research. Give yourself time. You do not want to be pressured or stressed the night before your speech. Allow yourself time—just in case the research indicates that you need to revise your position.

**Record Where You Found the Information:** make a preliminary bibliography. This will help you to keep track of your sources. This is a good idea in case you copied the information incorrectly. Without the bibliography you would have to sort through and read all the research documents again.

**Take Notes:** write out the information that you want to include. Place it on an index card. This will allow you to try different arrangements without having to write it all over again.

Think about your material as you do your research. Research is not a mechanical process. You should think about the information that you are gathering. Does it enhance, support or complement my objective? If it doesn't then you don't need it. If the information will clarify, support or enhance your speech then it should be included. In doing research you will come across a lot of interesting information but your job is to sift through it all and only pick out what is most useful and helpful to your speech.

# Chapter 9 Classroom Exercises

**Assignment 1**
Go back to one of your prior speeches. List the information that you know. Organize it. List the gaps that you have in your speech.

**Assignment 2**
Use the same speech above. List place where you can find the missing information. If on the internet, list the key words that you will use in your search.

**Assignment 3**
You are preparing a speech for which you need comments and feedback from your target audience. Devise a questionnaire (of about 5 questions). The questions should help you strengthen your position in your speech. Ask 5 of your classmates to participate in your survey.

## Chapter 9 Review

1. **Why is it good to start your research early?**

2. **Why should you take good notes?**

3. **Why should your record your sources?**

4. **List a few places where you can do research?**

## Research

5. **Why is it important to draw on your own knowledge and experience as you gather information for a speech?**

# Homework 9

### Assignment 1
Use the information from the classroom exercises assignment 2. Do the research. List your sources. Make detailed notes.

### Assignment 2
Using the information gathered in homework assignment 1. List whether you will use statistics, facts, stories, anecdotes etc. to strengthen your speech. Write what you will include. Incorporate it into your speech.

### Assignment 3
You are preparing a speech for which you need comments and feedback from your target audience. Devise a questionnaire (of about 5 questions). The questions should help you strengthen your position in your speech. Ask 5 people (family or friends) to participate in your survey. Compare the results you got from your classmates in class exercise 3. Does it support your position? Does it indicate you may have to revise your position? What conclusions can you draw?

## Self-Assessment Review 9

It's important to be able to assess your own presentations. You will not always get feedback from a relative, friend, classmate or an audience participant. You need to develop a habit of self-reflection and analysis. As a way of helping you develop this ability please answer the following questions.

**1. How would you rate your presentation on a scale of 1-10 (ten being exceptionally well)?**

**2. What are the mistakes you think you made?**

**3. What would you like to do better?**

**4. Did you communicate your point clearly to your audience?**

**5. Did your audience look engaged? Or confused?**

## Preview
In chapter 10, you will learn how to choose and use visual aids.

# Chapter 10

## Are Visual Aids Necessary?

*"Congressman Kucinich is holding up a pie chart, which is not truly effective on radio."*

—Neal Conan, Moderator

Are visual aids necessary? Not in all speeches. Are they helpful?—you bet.

**The Purpose of Visual Aids**
Visual aids have several advantages: they help to clarify information, they make the abstract concrete, they can stimulate interest, and they can help the audience to retain the information. They can also help you with your nervousness. But above all else they help to save time.

When giving a speech you don't want to make your audience has to work too hard to understand you. You want them to understand what you are saying and to follow your logic. Visual aids can help you achieve this. So the question now is what visual aids should you use?

The truth is that you will need to decide this for yourself. What will help you decide is the type of presentation you will be doing—is it a lecture or question and answer session, who your audience is—students, constituents, church members, and where the presentation will take place—in an auditorium, at your work place, in your church, in the park or at a town hall meeting. You would need to find out in advance if the facility will be able to accommodate your visual aid (equipment).

Once you know this you can decide on which type of display would work best.

Here are some options to choose from.

**Visual Aid Tools:**
- The Speaker: performing sign language
- Displays
  - Drawings: diagrams and sketches

# Are Visual Aids Necessary?

- Photographs: like old war pictures
- Graphs: these help to clarify statistics
- Charts
- Maps
- Transparencies
- Flip Charts

- White board Charts
- PowerPoint
    - Slides and movies
    - Computer based aids
    - Sound effects
    - Samples
- Handouts
    - Objects (things your audience can touch): like a guitar

## Visual Aid Tips
- Prepare in advance
- Avoid using a chalkboard (you will be too busy with your speech to set up the drawing properly—unless this is done in advance.)
- Make the visual aid large enough so that the last person in the last aisle, in the last seat can see it without difficulty
- Display the visual aid where all listeners can see it
- Don't block the visual aid
- Don't write as you speak
- Display the right visual aid
- Don't distract the listener. Do not pass around the visual aid or hand out while you are speaking. This take the attention off our speech and places it onto the visual aid
- Talk to your audience and not to your visual aid
- Display your visual aid only when you are referring to them
- Practice doing your speech with your visual aid
- Have them read and have a backup plan in case.... Be prepared in case something goes wrong with your visual aid
- Choose the best visual aid for the occasion
- Make sure in advance that the facility can accommodate your aid—especially if you are using laptops or other technical equipment

## Chapter 10 Classroom Exercises

**Assignment 1**
Bring in your visual aid. You will give your speech in front of your class. They will give you feedback on the effectiveness of your visual aid choice and offer suggestions or praise.

**Assignment 2**
If something goes wrong with your visual aid. What is your back up plan? Describe what you would do.

# Chapter 10 Review

1. Why are visual aids helpful?

2. What are the visuals aids you might use in your speech?

3. List the tips for using visuals aids.

## Homework 10

### Assignment 1
Go over one of your past speeches, and incorporate a visual aid to it. Practice using the visual aid.

### Assignment 2
Choose two different visual aids and incorporate them into your speech. Practice using them.

### Assignment 3
Compare the (two to four visual aids). Which one (s) enhanced your speech the best? Why do you feel this is so? Get feedback from a friend or relative. Did they confirm that your choice of visual aid helped them to retain the information? Did it clarify the information? Did it spark their interest? Or did it make your abstract concepts more concrete?

## Self-Assessment Review 10

It's important to be able to assess your own presentations. You will not always get feedback from a relative, friend, classmate or an audience participant. You need to develop a habit of self-reflection and analysis. As a way of helping you develop this ability please answer the following questions.

1. **How would you rate your presentation on a scale of 1-10 (ten being exceptionally well)?**

2. **What are the mistakes you think you made?**

3. **What would you like to do better?**

4. **Did you communicate your point clearly to your audience?**

5. **Did your audience look engaged? Or confused?**

## Preview
In chapter 11, you will learn if you have the gift of persuasion.

# Chapter 11

## Do You Have the Gift of Persuasion?

*Life is in the mouth; death is in the mouth.*

—Anonymous

Do you have a natural gift to persuade people to do what you want them to do? Or are you like many others who have to work at being persuasive? No matter which category you fit into the following tips will ensure that you are your persuasive best.

As I mentioned in chapter 3, speech organization, you need to know your audience. What are their thoughts, beliefs, attitudes, needs, problems, interests, and goals? Once you have this information you will apply it to your **target** audience (those who you want to persuade.)

Let me say this, you will never be able to convince everyone in your speech. Some listeners will be against your position no matter what you say or do. While others may already be in agreement with your position. Yet others may be undecided or simply don't care one way or another.

Your job is to set your sights on your target—the ones you want to reach the most, then aim and fire your best shot (presentation).

### The 911 on Persuasion
There are three types of persuasive speeches: those that convince, those that call to action, and those that inspire. Martin Luther King Jr.'s speech inspired people and incited them to action. A politician's speech will try to convince and call the listener to action.
As you can see a speech can accomplish more than one task.

### Methods of Persuasion
What are the methods of persuasion? How do you convince people of your position, beliefs, argument if they don't agree with you already?

# Do You Have the Gift of Persuasion?

There are four things that can help you to be a persuasive speaker...**credibility, evidence, reasoning and emotion.** Let us look at each on in depth.

**Credibility** as defined in the American Heritage College Dictionary is the quality, capability, or power to elicit belief. In other words, it is your ability to get people to believe that what you are saying is true. How can you do this?

You could wave a magic wand or try to hypnotize them into believing you...but it probably won't work. Or you could demonstrate it through your **competence and character.** Your audience wants to know that they are listening to someone who is knowledgeable and has intelligence on the subject matter. That alone will establish your credibility. Would you take advice on heart surgery from a comedian? Or a doctor with a medical degree?

Your character also helps to establish your credibility. Do you appear sincere, trustworthy, honest, and truthful? Do you show the audience that you care and are concerned about them? If you can communicate this to your audience, then you'll be well on your way to solidifying your credibility with them.

**Stages of Credibility**
**Initial Credibility**—the credibility that you have as the speaker before you start to speak.

**Derived Credibility**—the credibility that you have because of what you say or do during the speech.

**Terminal Credibility**—your credibility as the speaker at the end of your speech.

You can gain or lose your credibility through each stage of your speech. And yes, you can lose your credibility before you utter a word. How are you dressed? How did you approach the stage? What is your body posture communicating? These are the nonverbal things that can affect your credibility. (Please return to chapter 7 to learn more on how your body speaks.)

**Evidence** as defined in the American Heritage College Dictionary, is a thing or things helpful in forming a conclusion or judgment. In other words, what are you going to use to convince people that what you are saying has merit?

It is more effective to persuade an audience using evidence than without it. They want to know what you know you can prove or substantiate. Think CSI (the popular crime show on Channel 2) they gather evidence so they can solve the crime and make their case in court. You have to make your case to your audience—and the best way for you to do this **is with proof**.

What types of evidence are acceptable and helpful? As you will recall from chapter 9 testimonies, statistical facts and examples are evidence that will support your ideas, theories and your speech. Use them as you would salt on your food—sparingly...too much of one thing is good for nothing. The idea is not to overwhelm the audience or to bombard them with fact they may already know. It's to persuade them that what you are saying is true and so it should be believed.

**Reasoning** as defined by the American Heritage College Dictionary is the use of reason to form conclusions, inferences or judgments. Your audience will use reason to draw conclusions about your speech. That is why it is vital for you to give them enough information so they can conclude what you want them to.

In other words, you should know their arguments and resistance points and have an answer that will defuse their argument. In order to do this you would need to do research and know your target audience.

Reasoning is used in all aspects of our daily lives. It is an important element to critical thinking. That is why your reasoning should be sound. Once it is it will make convincing your listeners of this fact easier.

The truth is that no matter how strong your evidence is...you will not persuade your audience if they don't grasp your reasoning. It would be like trying to see in front of you when the fog is twelve inches thick.

There are several types of reasoning. Let us touch on them briefly.

**Deductive Reasoning** is reasoning from a general premise to a minor premise.

**Inductive Reasoning** is reasoning from a minor premise to a general premise.

**Casual Reasoning** is establishing a relationship between cause and effect.

# Do You Have the Gift of Persuasion?

**Analogical Reasoning** a comparison of similar situations and inferring that what is true in one must be true in the other.

I think at this point it would be beneficial to illustrate how each of these types of reasoning is different.

## Examples
### Deductive Reasoning
Women were created to have children
B. Paula is a woman.
C. Therefore Paula wants to have children.

In this instance you take a general belief and make it individual specific. Paula may not want to have children even though she has the ability to do so. Now let's look at inductive reasoning.

### Inductive Reasoning
A. My statistics class last fall was boring.
B. My girlfriend's statistics class was boring.
C. My sister's statistics class was boring.
D. Conclusion: Statistics classes are boring.

Inductive reasoning works in the opposite of deductive reasoning. As you can see we took several specific experiences and drew a general conclusion. Statistics may not be boring...it could be that all three unfortunately had boring teachers.

### Casual Reasoning
A. There is a crack on the side walk.
B. You fall and break your leg.
C. Conclusion: because of the crack on the side walk I broke my leg.

Could this be true? Yes. Could it be false? Yes. You could have fallen because of the crack, or because your shoes were big, or your foot was not in the proper alignment. But what you have just tried to do is to establish a cause and effect through casual reasoning.

### Analogical Reasoning
A. You are good at building model cars.
B. Therefore you will be a great mechanic.

In analogical reasoning you try to infer that because you are good at one thing then you will be good at another. Would you like a model car builder to be your mechanic?

As you can see from these reasoning plays an important part in our ability to persuade. You don't want to leave it up to your listener to decide what they will conclude alone. You want to give them a helping hand. Connect the dots loosely for them—by supplying the needed information and proof.

The last thing to help you be a persuasive speaker is the element of emotion. What is the emotional trigger you want to press—fear, pride, compassion, envy, anger, shame, greed, reverence, compassion, empathy? Whatever it is you have to press it hard until your listener responds the way that you want him to.

This is what advertisers do. Do you always want that ice cream at 10 o'clock at night? Or that chocolate fudge? No! But the advertisers knew how to press your button. Was it hunger; a need to be pampered; to feel comforted, or a need to feel good all over?

No matter what the emotional grab was, it worked—and that is what you want to do to your audience.

## Chapter 11 Classroom Exercises

**Assignment 1**
Create a profile of a speaker that would establish credibility. Write one paragraph of a speaker's speech. Present it to the class.

**Assignment 2**
Visualize your ideal audience and the message you want to convey to them. Outline the emotional triggers you will use. Write one paragraph showing how you will use emotion in your speech.

**Assignment 3**
Write a scenario (situation). Tell which type of reasoning could be applied to the scenario. Now outline how you would want your listener to reason this scenario if she was part of your target audience.

## Chapter 11 Review
Let's review what we have learned in this chapter.

1. **What are the key components to persuasion?**

2. **Why is character important to your audience?**

3. **What role does evidence play in a speech?**

4. **What are the types of reasoning?**

5. **What role does emotion play in the art of persuasion?**

6. **List a few of the emotional triggers that you can press as a speaker.**

7. **What is the target audience?**

## Homework 11
Below I have included one of my speeches. You will analyze it for evidence, tone, emotion, credibility, and target audience.

## Life's Two Buckets
Do you believe that as a public speaker, you have the power to breathe life or destruction with the words you chose use?

Well you do.

In life you carry two buckets. One bucket is filled with water and the other is filled with gasoline. And each day you have a choice of which bucket you will use in any given situation.

**For example:** when your son tells you he wants to be an inventor when he grows up. Do you encourage him by pouring on the gasoline?

*"John I know that you'll invent things that will help people's lives to be better."*

Or do you pour on the water...

*"How can you become an inventor—look at your grades. It would be a wonder if you make it out of the seventh grade."*

But there are other situations where you are required to make a choice about which bucket you will use.

For instance when your spouse, co-worker, church brethren, friend or relative get on your last nerve. And all he or she is doing is complaining and finding fault with everything you do or say.

Do you choose to throw water on the situation—thus putting out the fire? Or do you pour on the gas—and give him or her the "what not's"?

Here...

But since this is a speaking club let us explore how the choices you make about which bucket to use can benefit or hurt your fellow Toastmasters club members.

Let's say that one of your fellow Toastmaster's has given a speech. Her hair was disheveled. Throughout her speech she clicked her tongue. Her speech was disorganized and she pronounced simple words incorrectly.

Which bucket will you choose to pour?

Keep in mind you are irritated and annoyed because you feel she has wasted your valuable time.

Do you chose the water bucket...you would encourage her by giving her tips on how she can constructively improve her speech for the next time.

But—suppose you chose the gas bucket.

You'd let her know how much you hated her speech, and that you are disappointed in her because she was not prepared and she mispronounced simple words. In other words you let her have it.

Now... you feel better because you let out all your venom on her. But she is so devastated that she starts to cry as she picks up her belongings to leave.

Granted no one in here would think to be so cruel to a fellow Toastmaster...but when you speak choose to pour water or gas on a situation make sure that it serves the best possible purpose.

If you want to head off a potentially explosive situation choose water. If you want to encourage someone to follow his or her dreams or to strive for an achievement then chose the gas.

And if by chance you're not sure which to use...then wait.

As public speakers you have the potential to encourage, support, teach, or crush people with the words you chose to use. And the way in which you deliver them.

Please don't take your power lightly. And yes, you heard me correctly—I said power! You have the power to breathe life into a situation or a person. Or to destroy a person's hopes and dreams. And you can do this with a simple choice of which bucket you choose to use.

Use life's two buckets wisely...it's an awesome responsibility.

# Do You Have the Gift of Persuasion?

**Assignment 1**
Analyze Life Two Buckets for evidence. List the evidence below.

**Assignment 2**
Analyze the above speech for emotion. List what you find below.

**Assignment 3**
Analyze it for the target audience.

**Assignment 4**
Analyze it for credibility or character.

## Self-Assessment Review 11

It's important to be able to assess your own presentations. You will not always get feedback from a relative, friend, classmate or an audience participant. You need to develop a habit of self-reflection and analysis. As a way of helping you develop this ability please answer the following questions.

1. **How would you rate your presentation on a scale of 1-10 (ten being exceptionally well)?**

2. **What are the mistakes you think you made?**

3. **What would you like to do better?**

4. **Did you communicate your point clearly to your audience?**

5. **Did your audience look engaged? Or confused?**

## Preview

In chapter 12, you will learn about how you can inspire your audience.

# Chapter 12

## Can You Inspire Your Audience?

*The basic rule of human nature is that powerful people speak slowly and subservient people quickly --because if they don't speak fast nobody will listen to them.*

—Michael Caine

Are you ready to learn how to inspire your audience? How to call them to action or to convince them? You basically understand how to do this already. Even if you don't feel like you do.

In order to inspire your audience you first need to connect with them—on some level. There are five human needs according to Psychologist Abraham Maslow that you can use to connect with your audience. They are physiological needs, safety needs, belongingness and love, esteem—self-esteem and self-actualization.

Let's look at each one of these more in depth.

**Physiological Needs**
These are the things you need to survive—air, food, water, sleep, shelter, and warmth.

**Safety Needs**
These are the things you need to feel secure and protected—security, stability.

**Belongingness and Love**
This is being accepted, a part of a group.

**Esteem—self-esteem**
This is having self-confidence, self-respect, status, independence or competence.

**Self-actualization**
This is the realization of potential and self-fulfillment.

If you can tap into these needs you will be able to inspire your audience. In this chapter you will spend more time on exercises so that we can properly drive home the point.

## Chapter 12 Classroom Exercises

**Assignment 1**
You are planning to give a speech to a group of high school students about interview skills. How would you establish a bond with them?

**Assignment 2**
You are planning to give a speech to group real estate agents. You want them to increase their sales. How would you establish a bond with them?

**Assignment 3**
You are planning to give a speech to a group of parents who lost a child because of gun violence. How would you establish a bond with them?

# Chapter 12 Review

1. **What are the five human needs?**

2. **Describe the five human needs.**

# Homework 12

## Assignment 1
You are a business executive. You are having a meeting with your staff about productivity. There have been rumors of lay-offs. You want your staff to increase productivity. What would you say to them?

## Assignment 2
You are giving a commencement speech. You want to inspire the students. What would you say to them?

## Assignment 3
You are running for political office. You want to win. What would you do and say in order to convince people you are the right person for the job?

## Self-Assessment Review 12

It's important to be able to assess your own presentations. You will not always get feedback from a relative, friend, classmate or an audience participant. You need to develop a habit of self-reflection and analysis. As a way of helping you develop this ability please answer the following questions.

**1. How would you rate your presentation on a scale of 1-10 (ten being exceptionally well)?**

**2. What are the mistakes you think you made?**

**3. What would you like to do better?**

**4. Did you communicate your point clearly to your audience?**

**5. Did your audience look engaged? Or confused?**

## Preview

In chapter 13, you will discover how well you listen when people speak.

# Chapter 13

# How Well Do You Listen?

*Listen not merely to what is said but to the tone of voice in which it is said.*

—Anonymous

Did you know that you spend more time listening then you do speaking? Did you know that people who listen well are better public speakers? Did you know that there is a difference between hearing and listening?

Well, research has found that the ability to listen well has a dramatic impact on how well one does as a speaker. And it has also shown that most people are poor listeners...and so it stands to reason that most people are poor public speakers.

I would like to give you a pop quiz. There is no need to answer this question out loud but you should answer them in your mind...and please, please be honest with yourself.

When you are listening to a speaker, do you get distracted? Does your mind wonder? Do you start to think of all the other places you would rather be or the things you would rather be doing?

Do you jump to conclusions before the speaker has had the chance to state what he or she wanted to say? In other words to do you put your words into the speakers mouth?

Do you listen too closely to each and every word that the speaker says...because you believe each word has equal importance?

Do you judge the value, quality, or importance of a speech based on how the speaker looks, sounds or what the speaker does?

If you answered yes to all or just one of these questions you are a poor listener!

# How Well Do You Listen?

Listening is a skill that requires you to do more than just hear the words a speaker uses. It requires that you pay attention, pick out the speakers main points, and grasp the speaker's purpose for the speech.

And this will be difficult to do if you are distracted, judgmental, dismissive, or if you focus too hard on each word.

Okay so you're a poor listener...is all hope lost?

No. Listening is like any other skill it can be improved with practice and self-discipline.

But only people who take listening seriously will improve. You see there is another group of people out there. Those that like to be heard. They want to speak for they know everything and are not willing to learn or be persuaded. These are people are "talkers".

I'm sure you've met the type... no matter what you are saying they chime in with their pre-rehearsed conversation and they "throw up" all over you. And often they leave you feeling yucky, or confused or insulted.

But I know you're not like that! You are a Master Public Speaker in Training and you are interested in anything that can help you improve your public speaking skills.

So the question now is how can you improve your listening skills? It's simple. Be serious. Resist. Suspend. Refuse. Focus.

### Be Serious about Listening
Decide that listening is serious and worth the effort.

### Resist Distractions
Choose not to give in to distracting thoughts when people are speaking.

### Suspend Judgment
Wait until you have more information before your judge the quality, usefulness, and importance of the speech. You may learn something or be persuaded.

**Refuse to be Diverted by Appearance or Delivery**
Don't dismiss the speaker or his message because of appearance or delivery. Listen to the message…for most speeches have beneficial information within them.

**Focus Your Listening**
Listen for main points, evidence, technique, and take notes. As you listen to co-workers, family members and friends purpose to resist, suspend, refuse, and focus. When you do this daily, you will increase your listening skills and it will sharpen your speaking skills as well. It will remove assumptions. It will help you to better clarify issues. It will enable you to target your response properly. It will make you strategic and purposeful in your communications and these are the skills you need to be a Master Public Speaker.

So the only question I have for you is …do you plan to be serious about listening?

# Chapter 13 Classroom Exercises

Please use the informal speech evaluation form in the back of the book to complete assignments 1 to 3.

**Assignment 1**
For this assignment you are to listen to a speech from one of your classmates. You will have two minutes to write down your thought about his/her speech. You are to put into practice what you have learned in this chapter about listening.

**Assignment 2**
For this assignment you are to listen to a speech from one of your classmates. You will have two minutes to write down your thought about his/her speech. You are to put into practice what you have learned in this chapter about listening.

**Assignment 3**
For this assignment you are to listen to a speech from one of your classmates. You will have two minutes to write down your thought about his/her speech. You are to put into practice what you have learned in this chapter about listening.

## Assignment 4

Please go over assignments 1-3 and answer the following questions. You can use your evaluation notes that you took during and after the speech presentation.

1. **Did you find it difficult to concentrate on the speech?**

2. **What made it the most difficult for you?**

3. **Which speech did you enjoy the most?**

4. **Which speech was the most memorable?**

5. **Which speech did you have the most negative reaction to? Why?**

6. **Which speaker left you with the most positive feeling?**

7. **Which speaker left you with the most negative feeling?**

## Chapter 13 Review

1. **Why should you be serious about listening?**

2. **How can you focus your listening?**

3. **How can judgment affect your listening?**

4. **How can a speaker's appearance effect your listening if you are not careful?**

# Homework 13

## Assignment 1
Turn to your favorite news channel and watch a five minute segment of the anchors presentation. Please note the time, channel, anchor's name and the topic he is discussing. Write out in detail what you learned from the anchors presentation.

## Assignment 2
For the next two days I want you to observe yourself as you listen to people around you talk. Record what turns you off, what helps you to listen better, are you actively listening or just acting like you are. Record the type of conversation, who is speaking to you, how long it lasted (approximately), and your reaction to it.

## Assignment 3
Flesh out assignment 2 some more. Did the speaker know that you had any negative reactions to the conversation? Did you feel good about how you were listening in the conversation? Were you able to respond appropriately or did you have to ask the speaker to repeat what he said?

## Self-Assessment Review 13

It's important to be able to assess your own presentations. You will not always get feedback from a relative, friend, classmate or an audience participant. You need to develop a habit of self-reflection and analysis. As a way of helping you develop this ability please answer the following questions.

1. **How would you rate your presentation on a scale of 1-10 (ten being exceptionally well)?**

2. **What are the mistakes you think you made?**

3. **What would you like to do better?**

4. **Did you communicate your point clearly to your audience?**

5. **Did your audience look engaged? Confused?**

## Preview
Conclusion.

# Conclusion

To be a Master Public Speaker it important to be yourself—don't try to be someone else for you are unique and special. Make sure that you give your audience a reason to pay attention to your message—do your research it will go a long way to building your credibility. Convey your message in a clear way—don't allow your audience to get confused because they will tune you out.

Dress to impress— dress appropriately for the occasion. And remember to enjoy the process—you will learn so much about yourself if you go in with the right outlook.

## Preview

As promised I have included a bonus section in it you will find **10 Public Speaking Mistakes You Want to Avoid...at All Costs, 9 Keys for Public Speaking Success** and *seven* evaluation templates.

# References

Bono, Edward. Teach Your Child to Think, New York; Penguin Books, 1994.

Dyett-Welcome, Michelle. Excuse Me! Let Me Speak...A Young Persons Guide to Public Speaking, Indiana; AuthorHouse, 2009.

Lucas, Stephen E. The Art of Public Speaking, 3rd ed., New York; Random House, 1989.

Mack, Knox, McGalliard, Pasinetti, Hugo, Spacks, Wellek, Douglas, Lawall. The Norton Anthology of World Masterpieces, vol. II, 5th ed., New York; W.W. Norton & Company, 1985.

O'Shaughnessy, J., and Nicholas Jackson O'Shaughnessy. The Marketing Power of Emotion, New York; Oxford University Press, 2003.

Sugarman, Joseph. Triggers, Las Vegas; DelStar Books 1999.

Wilkie, Brian, and James Hurt. Literature of the Western World, vol. I, New York; MacMillan Publishing Company, 1988.

# Bonus Section

In this section you will find the 10 public speaking mistakes you want to avoid, the 9 keys to success, plus **seven** evaluation templates. All templates can be reproduced for your personal use.

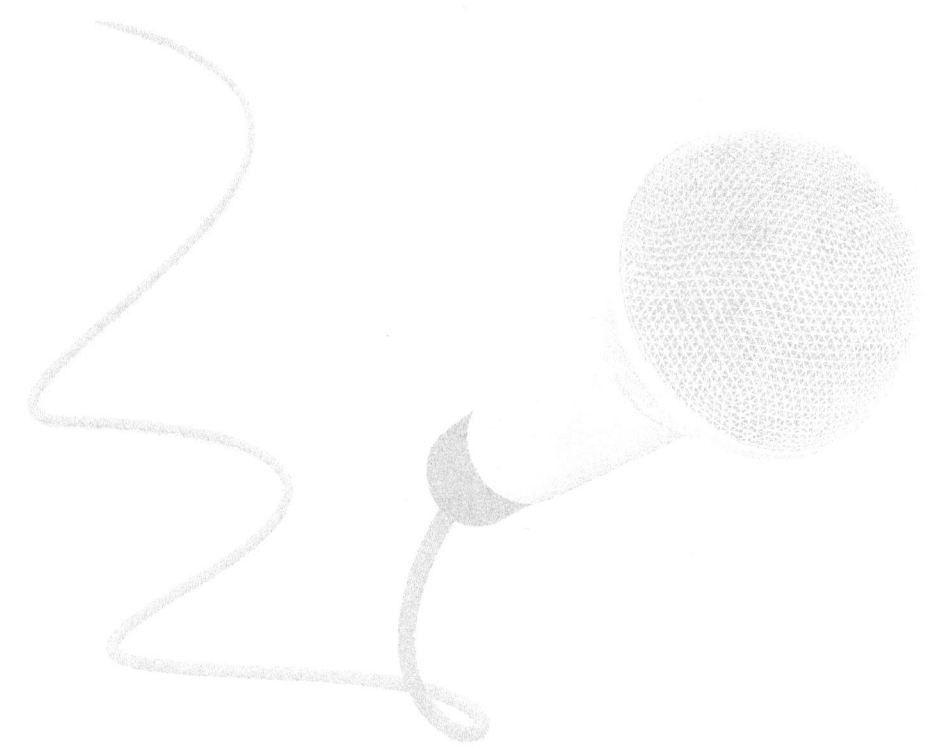

## 10 Public Speaking Mistakes You Want to Avoid ...At ALL Costs...

1. Using um's in your speech
2. Using ah's in your speech
3. Using the phrase "you know"
4. Excessive hand or foot movements
5. Constantly running your hands through your hair
6. Making clicking sounds with your tongue or lips
7. Not making eye contact with your audience
8. Speaking in a whisper
9. Using a monotone voice
10. Not engaging your audience (with questions, jokes, or a story)

## 9 Keys for Public Speaking Success

1. Make it personal
2. Make it interesting
3. Don't be a slave to formality
4. Be conversational
5. Address your audiences "what's" within your speech
6. Eliminate indifference
7. Overcome skepticism
8. Use quotes and facts to establish credibility
9. Get your audience to respond

Bonus Section

# The SMART (Informal) Speech Evaluation Form (Template)

| Observations | Done Well | Could Use Improvement | Suggestions for Improvement |
|---|---|---|---|
| **Non-Verbal Communications** | | | |
| Appearance | | | |
| Body Language | | | |
| Posture | | | |
| Distracting Habits | | | |
| Eye Contact | | | |
| Smiled (connected with audience) | | | |
| **Preparation** | | | |
| Organization | | | |
| Clear Opening | | | |
| New terms Defined | | | |
| Sound Reasoning | | | |
| Emphasized Key facts and ideas | | | |
| **Delivery** | | | |
| Voice | | | |
| Enunciation | | | |
| Modulation | | | |
| Speed | | | |
| Showed Emotion | | | |
| Generated Emotion | | | |
| Strong and memorable closing | | | |

# The SMART Ah/Um Record
## (Template)

| Program Section | Ah's | Um's | So's | "You Knows" |
|---|---|---|---|---|
| **Class Exercises** | | | | |
| 1. | | | | |
| 2. | | | | |
| 3. | | | | |
| 4. | | | | |
| 5. | | | | |
| **Homework Exercises** | | | | |
| 1. | | | | |
| 2. | | | | |
| 3. | | | | |
| 4. | | | | |
| 5. | | | | |
| **Evaluators** | | | | |
| 1. | | | | |
| 2. | | | | |
| 3. | | | | |
| 4. | | | | |
| 5. | | | | |
| | | | | |
| **General Evaluator** | | | | |
| 1. | | | | |
| | | | | |
| **Timer** | | | | |
| 1. | | | | |

Bonus Section

# The SMART General Evaluator
## (Template)

**Date:** _____

Give a brief description of your role as the General Evaluator. Try to include your purpose, why the evaluation process is beneficial to the members, what the process will entail and any techniques that will be used during this phase of the program.

Note: The evaluation team includes the grammarian, ah-counter, timer, and the speech evaluators.

When it is time for your general evaluation comments, you should consider some of the following.

| Suggested Items to Evaluate | Your Thoughts |
|---|---|
| Did the meeting start on time? | |
| Uses the club banner? | |
| What went well in the meeting? | |
| What can be improved? | |
| Where there any distractions or interruption in the meeting? | |
| Did the meeting transition from one section to the other smoothly? | |
| How did the other members generally perform their duties? | |
| Did the program go according to the time constraints? | |
| Other comments and observations. | |

**Note:** A General Evaluator is the person who evaluates each section of the evening's program.

Bonus Section

# The SMART Self-Assessment Review
## (Template)

It's important to be able to assess your own presentations. You will not always get feedback from a relative, friend, classmate or an audience participant. You need to develop a habit of self-reflection and analysis. As a way of helping you develop this ability please answer the following questions.

1. How would you rate your presentation on a scale of 1-10 (ten being exceptionally well)?

2. What are the mistakes you think you made?

3. What would you like to do better?

4. Did you communicate your point clearly to your audience?

5. Did your audience look engaged? Or confused?

The Smart Guide to Public Speaking

# The SMART Timer's Record

| Program Section | Time Requirement | Officially Recorded Time | Finished on Time | Went Over |
|---|---|---|---|---|
| **Start of Meeting** | | | | |
| **End of Meeting** | | | | |
| **Class Speakers** | | | | |
| 1. | | | | |
| 2. | | | | |
| 3. | | | | |
| 4. | | | | |
| 5. | | | | |
| **Evaluators** | | | | |
| 1. | | | | |
| 2. | | | | |
| 3. | | | | |
| 4. | | | | |
| 5. | | | | |

### Timing Table

| Timing | Green | Yellow | Red |
|---|---|---|---|
| Assignment Speech | 2:00 | 2:30 | 3:00 |
| Evaluations | 2:00 | 2:30 | 3:00 |

Bonus Section

# The SMART (Informal) Speech Evaluation Form
## (Template)

| Observations | Done Well | Could Use Improvement | Suggestions for Improvement |
|---|---|---|---|
| **Non-Verbal Communications** | | | |
| Appearance | | | |
| Body Language | | | |
| Posture | | | |
| Distracting Habits | | | |
| Eye Contact | | | |
| Smiled (connected with audience) | | | |
| **Preparation** | | | |
| Organization | | | |
| Clear Opening | | | |
| New terms Defined | | | |
| Sound Reasoning | | | |
| Emphasized Key facts and ideas | | | |
| **Delivery** | | | |
| Voice | | | |
| Enunciation | | | |
| Modulation | | | |
| Speed | | | |
| Showed Emotion | | | |
| Generated Emotion | | | |
| Strong and memorable closing | | | |

The Smart Guide to Public Speaking

# The SMART Evaluation of the Speaker Form
## (Template)

**Presentation Date:**
**Presentation Topic:**
**Presentation Speaker:**

**Evaluator:**
**Greetings Mr. /Madam, fellow classmates, most welcomed guests, and especially
_____.**

**I.** These are the things I felt you did well in your presentation:

    Tone          Emotional connection         Speech Organization
    Volume       Emphasized important points  Use of story
    Clarity        Posture (body gestures)      Use of humor
    Pace          Eye contact               Use of questions to engage
    Use of space around the lectern

**Additional Thoughts:**

**II.** With all the great things that you did in your presentation there are a few things that if improved I believe it will increase the effectiveness and impact of your presentation:

    Tone          Emotional connection         Speech Organization
    Volume       Emphasized important points  Use of story
    Clarity        Posture (body gestures)      Use of humor
    Use of questions to engage the audience  Pace
    Didn't need to use notes as much        Eliminate the Ok's
    Eliminate the Um's

**Additional Thoughts:**

III. But I must admit that I found your:

    Topic           Enthusiasm          Emphasis
    Person ability   Confidence          Delivery

**Additional Thoughts:**

**Thank you Mr./ Madam**

Bonus Section

# The SMART Speakers Final Project Evaluation Form
## (For judges)

Date: _____

Speaker: _____

| Observatons | Excellent | ___ | Average | ___ | None | Score |
|---|---|---|---|---|---|---|
| | 20 | 15 | 10 | 5 | 0 | |
| ***Non-Verbal Communications*** | | | | | | |
| Appearance | | | | | | |
| Body Language | | | | | | |
| Posture | | | | | | |
| Distracting Habits | | | | | | |
| Eye Contact | | | | | | |
| Smile (connected with audience) | | | | | | |
| ***Preparation*** | | | | | | |
| Organization | | | | | | |
| Clear Opening | | | | | | |
| New Terms Defined | | | | | | |
| Sound Reasoning | | | | | | |
| Emphasized Key Facts & Ideas | | | | | | |
| ***Delivery*** | | | | | | |
| Voice | | | | | | |
| Enunciation | | | | | | |
| Modulation | | | | | | |
| Speed | | | | | | |
| Showed Emotion | | | | | | |
| Generated Emotion | | | | | | |
| Strong Memorable Closing | | | | | | |
| | | | | | Total Score | |

# About the Author

**Michelle J. Dyett-Welcome** is the author of *Excuse Me! Let Me Speak...A Young Persons Guide to Public Speaking* and *The Excuse Me! Let Me Speak... A Young Persons Guide to Public Speaking Teacher's Manual.*

She is a professional speaker, copywriter and the president of S.M.A.R.T. Copy Designs Inc. (http://smartcopydesignsinc.com).

She lives in Far Rockaway, New York, with her husband, Dwain, and their two children, Maheem and Matteel, along with their three cats—Silver, Buttons, and Shadow—and their pet dog, Peaches.

To learn more about public speaking visit http://excusemeletmespeak.com/.